Ghost Hunting
The
Spiritual
Way

First edition, September 2010

Printed and bound in the United Kingdom

ISBN: 978-1-4461-8828-6

Ghost-Hunting
The
Spiritual
Way

By
Former

Most Haunted
Resident Medium

Chris Conway

This book is dedicated to my wonderful family Carole-Anne, Chris Jnr, Ricky, Alicia, Kayla, Eva & Jessica. You guys are my inspiration and with you lot behind me I can achieve anything ☺

xxx

Table Of Contents

Look out for the subtle pebbles in life to help build your path of destiny.

- Chris Conway

Ghost-Hunting The Spiritual Way

__Introduction__

One of the first questions I'm always asked by people is: How can I get more out of my paranormal investigation without having to spend a fortune on equipment? In an ideal world everyone going on a ghost hunt would have a medium they could take along with them that they can trust. However, I believe that even having a good medium along to tell you who is around you and what they are doing doesn't let you fully immerse yourself in what I personally believe a ghost hunt should be about.

I believe a ghost hunt should be about using your own natural sensitivities to try and connect with whatever is in that location. Let the medium guide you and advise you but don't rely on him/her to do it all for you. If you allow this I feel that you are missing out on so much satisfaction and learning.

I am not saying here do not use any other ghost hunting equipment such as EMF metres etc. I am merely saying use them but also use your basic senses to tell you what is happening. So if you have no money start by learning the techniques shown in this book and buy your equipment gradually as you develop.

In this book I have tried to keep things as brief as possible. The reason for this is I want you to be able to use this book like an instruction manual for paranormal investigating. I didn't want it being so long and full of stuff not needed for an investigating that it put you off. I don't think paranormal investigating should be daunting and most certainly didn't want my book being daunting. Keeping it brief and straight to the point may seem easy but for me it was anything but. I am so passionate about the paranormal that when I start talking about it I don't stop for quite a while ☺.

The first part of this book will focus on the spirit world itself as I feel that it is very important to understand where spirit exists and a bit about what spirit is etc before you attempt to try and communicate with them.

The second part of the book is all about working on developing your own sensitivities. I will be teaching you various techniques and experiments to use in your own paranormal investigation. Again I feel that doing this can only enhance your experience of paranormal experience.

The next part will give the budding ghost hunter a brief overview of the scientific ghost hunting equipment that you see the professionals use and how to use it. This will be followed by looking at more spiritual Ghost hunting equipment such as Ouija Boards, Dowsing Rods etc. I will even be showing you how to make your own for next to no money at all ☺.

I will then be trying to explain how to tie it all together in an actual paranormal investigation. This will be followed by a few examples of investigations that I have been part of recently and where possible explain how I bring information through.

I have really enjoyed writing this book for you guys and I just hope you enjoy reading it. I would like to take this point to thank my facebook family for all of the love, support and encouragement they have given me to write it ☺

Blessings

Chris

The Spiritual Planes

Before we can even think about contacting spirit on our own or as part of a paranormal investigation I believe that it is important to understand where and how spirit exists. I am going to very briefly describe to you about the spiritual planes and what they are. I will speak more about them in my next book as I don't have the time or space in this book to do them proper justice. The spirit world (I include our world in this term… on reading this book you will understand why) is made up of a series of planes (in simple terms a plane is a realm of existence). We live in the bottom plane, which I call the physical plane. Here our spirit is carried about in a physical vessel called the human body. This body is only a temporary structure and will dissipate once the time comes for our spirit to leave this plane and move onto the next. This world is made up of energy which vibrates at a slower rate than the higher planes (thus its contents seem to be solid in structure).

Depending on how we live our 'life' on this physical plane we will move onto a higher plane. If we are evil on this plane then we will move onto the second plane which organised religion calls Hell. Once on this plane there is very little chance to climb to the higher planes. However, I have been told by spirit that it is not impossible. The Greater Energy is all good and anyone can change their ways (even on the second plane) and climb to the higher planes. However, many of these spirits are still as bad and evil as they were on this plane and don't want to climb to the higher planes. They don't want the goodness and freshness of these higher planes.

The third plane is where the rest of us begin our next journey. This is the plane where we begin to acclimatise to our new existence. This may take many months or many years depending on the spirit. This like the planes higher up is a beautiful place to spend time. It is everything we could wish for, and more, and is a place where we will begin to work with the spirit (mankind) on this plane. This work is in order to start to learn more about our spiritual selves and begin to climb the higher planes.

I will leave this here as I don't want to bog you down with too much detail as this book is about investigating apparent haunted locations not about spiritual evolution.

What are Spirits?

I think that before we go searching for the elusive spirits and ghosts we first have to know what exactly they are. Without this basic knowledge it would be like me giving an alien a bucket and asking him to go milk a cow… the sheep may wonder why this strange man is messing with her bits whilst balancing over a bucket ☺

The answer is actually very simple… at least it is to begin with. Spirit are us and we are spirit. As I said I have furnished you with a very simple answer that will probably mean nothing to most of you. When we are born the Greater Energy (I will discuss this more in my next book) provides us with a physical vessel (our body) to carry our spirit (also known as our mind) through the trials and tribulations of the first plane (our world). As I will describe later in this book these are two different entities sharing the same space with a third entity, the ego. When our time on this physical plane comes to an end only one of these entities, our spirit (mind) moves onto the higher planes (the spirit world). Now my original answer will make more sense... Spirit are us and we are spirit.

When the spirit (mind) moves on we lose five of our six senses and are left with the sixth sense. We lose the ability to taste, touch, hear, see and smell. When I say 'lose' I don't mean this in a bad way I mean that we discard them as we no longer need them as these are physical senses for a physical world. We are left with our sixth sense which is our spiritual sense. This is the sense that we as mediums use when communicating with spirit. Here spirit can communicate using the ability of telepathy, and much more (I will explain more about the sixth sense in my next book as I don't have the room to go into it in great detail in this one). You may well be shouting at the book, "*If spirit can't see and hear then how on earth are we supposed to believe that they can take part in a séance?*" To this I'd say very good question guys ☺. The answer to this is telepathy! They have the ability to reach deep inside our mind (spirit) and see and hear (in a telepathic sense) our thoughts. So when we are doing something we think about it without realising it. When we are looking at something we are thinking about it. When we speak we think it first, again without realising. So spirit see and hear this entire subconscious thought pattern in our mind (spirit) and this is how they continue to hear and see on the physical plane.

I feel that I have to point out here that when spirit leaves this physical plane and moves onto the spiritual planes he/she doesn't suddenly become Evil and nasty. Spirit keeps the same personality and likes and dislikes as they had on this plane. In other words a spirit who had a cutting and wicked sense of humour will carry this onto the higher planes. A spirit who hated people with black hair will continue to hate people with black hair. Thus, a good spirit whilst on this plane will continue to be a good spirit on the higher planes and a bad spirit on this plane will continue to be a bad spirit. I have even had spirit communicating with me and talking about football and telling me that they still come back every now and then and watch their favourite team. So this explains why certain spirits stay in 'haunted' houses. They love them so much they want to remain there. Others of course hated the place so much that they feel that they must keep going back there. A bit like the person verbally abused in their younger days will tend to seek out a partner who will keep this going (not always but studies have shown that this happens in many cases).

When we begin our paranormal investigating we also have to keep in mind that spirit will choose when they communicate with us and not us. This might seem common sense to many of you but people forget. It seems to be a common myth that if you antagonise spirit they will come out fighting and make loads of bad and evil stuff happen. This is a lot of rubbish and in fact the opposite will happen. They will ignore you and do nothing. Spirit aren't there as dancing monkeys for us investigators to come in and click our fingers whilst shouting, "perform you B******S!" This is disrespectful and downright rude. You wouldn't do it to a spirit still on this plane so don't do it to spirits on the higher planes. We must at all times be respectful to spirit and they will in turn be respectful back.

Evil Spirits

I know I said earlier in the book that not all spirits are evil but we have to remember that some of them are. Some are just as nasty as they were on this plane. I want to write a little about coming into contact with darker spirits.

The thing we have to remember is that darker spirits have no need to work with spirits (us) on our plane. They don't want to climb the higher planes and thus will try and scare and confuse us. Instead of telling us true information about themselves they will make up lies and play with our heads. They CANNOT hurt us physically, however; they can most definitely hurt us mentally. Don't panic though as this will only last as long as the spirit is in your presence and a good medium will protect you and ensure that spirit will not try and attach themselves to you. However, I should point out here that spirit have spent so long at a certain place because they have a bond with this location. So it is quite arrogant of us to think that a spirit would suddenly see our boring little lives as an ideal replacement to the place they have spent so much time and have such an affinity with the energy in that place.

A question I'm so often asked is, *"How do we know when a spirit is an evil spirit?"* My answer to this is that they tend to smell bad ☺. You will suddenly catch a whiff of a bad smell (unless the person beside you enjoyed a vindaloo and a few beers the night before). The feeling of the room also changes to a quite sinister, heavy feeling. It's hard to describe that change in energy on paper but you will know when you feel it.

What is the difference between a Spirit and a Ghost?

To me a spirit is an intelligent entity no matter what plane they are on. They have the ability to communicate with the spirits (us) on this plane and are aware of what is going on round about them. They still have all their traits that they had on this plane and still have likes and dislikes and so on.

A ghost on the other hand is, in my belief system, a recording of a past event. They are very much like a video recording or a picture in an old photograph album. They are not the spirit that was, merely a representation of an event from the past. They cannot interact with us and have no knowledge of our presence. The original spirit will be intelligent in some form in the higher planes but this is not them. In fact in theory they could actually stand in the location and watch the exact same re-enactment take place! How freaky is that a spirit watching its own ghost!

The Seven Major Chakras

Put simply Chakras are spiritual openings into which we receive energy to power our body. Each Chakra is associated with a particular part of our life and body.

These consist of seven major Chakras and 21 minor Chakras. There are also lots of miniature Chakras all over the body. In this part of the book I'll concentrate on the seven major Chakras and try to help you understand about them and the difference they can make to your spiritual development.

Even though these Chakras are separate spiritual openings they are all connected by a spiritual tube. I want you to imagine these openings as being like little whirl pools sucking energy into their particular area of the body. When successfully opened energy will come gushing into your body through that particular opening. Every Chakra has an opening and an exit and energy enters them in a particular direction. Thus, it is very important that we learn which direction energy enters that particular Chakra.

The following is a very basic description of the Chakras and what they represent and what colour is associated with them. Obviously this is just a starting point and they can be studied in much more detail. I will describe them further in my next book (surprise surprise ☺):

First Chakra: Base Chakra

Colour: Red.

Location: The base of the spine.

Direction: This Chakra runs from the base to the head drawing its energy up from the direction of the ground.

Description: This Chakra rules the physical earthly part of our being. This is all about how we interact with nature and what we put back to it. Do we appreciate what is all around us and the miracles it produces or are we totally unconscious to it all?

Second Chakra: Naval Chakra

Colour: Orange.

Location: Just below the naval.

Direction: This Chakra runs from the naval to the back and also from the back to the naval.

Description: This Chakra rules your non-sexual relationships with others. In other words are you capable of life-long friendships.

Third Chakra: Solar Plexus

Colour: Yellow.

Location: Below your breastbone and slightly to the left.

Direction: From the front to the back and the back to the front.

Description: This Chakra rules your will power and how determined you are to succeed in life. It is also believed that this Chakra controls your destiny.

Fourth Chakra: Heart Chakra

Colour: Green.

Location: In the middle of the breastbone above the chest.

Direction: In through the heart through the body to the back and in through the back through the body to the heart.

Description: This Chakra rules the unconditional love we have for the world and everyone in it. Certain peoples Chakras are opened more regularly than others ☺.

Fifth Chakra: Throat Chakra

Colour: Light Blue.

Location: The throat.

Direction: From the throat to the back and from the back to the throat.

Description: This Chakra controls the wisdom of speech. When I say this I mean that it controls when we say the right thing for the right situation and when to say nothing. I believe that this Chakra also rules our intuition.

Sixth Chakra: Third Eye Chakra

Colour: Purple.

Location: The middle of the forehead.

Direction: The third eye through the body and the back through the body.

Description: This Chakra is associated with the pituitary gland. I believe that this Chakra rules our psychic ability. This is where I, and many other people, believe the sixth sense is found.

Seventh Chakra: Crown Chakra

Colour: Some people believe the colour is violet and some people believe it is white. I personally believe it is white.

Location: The Crown of the Head.

Direction: This spiritual opening is at the top of the head and it draws energy in from this direction. In other words this is where we draw in cosmic energy.

Description: This Chakra rules self-realisation. In other words this rules the state that we all strive to attain. It is the state of 'Just being and knowing all'.

The first and seventh Chakras are constantly open and vibrating at a low density. The speed of vibration must be increased if we want to draw more energy into these. The other five Chakras are closed and we must open them up to draw in energy.

The two Chakras I feel will be useful opening for a paranormal investigation are the Third-eye and the Crown Chakras. I feel that these will facilitate your psychic experiences and help make you more sensitive to what's around you.

Opening The Third-Eye Chakra

- Concentrate on your breathing for 5 minutes.

- Deep breath in through your mouth and out through your nose.

- Once you feel thoroughly relaxed and at ease with your self and your surroundings (about 5 or 10 minutes) then you are ready for the next stage.

- Continue your deep breathing and concentrate on the centre of your forehead and at the same spot at the back of your head. Imagine the energy coming in through both of these spiritual openings. You may start to feel a slight tingling sensation just in front of these spots.

- Now imagine a ball of purple energy hovering in front of you. Really feel the colour. Vividly create it in your mind. Now imagine the purple come gushing in through your Third-Eye and engulfing the inside of your body in this purple energy.

- Feel how this purple energy makes you feel so alive and happy and invigorated.

- Continue to bathe in this energy for as long as you enjoy it ☺.

Opening The Crown Chakra

- Concentrate on your breathing for 5 minutes.

- Deep breath in through your mouth and out through your nose.

- Once you feel thoroughly relaxed and at ease with your self and your surroundings (about 5 or 10 minutes) then you are ready for the next stage.

- Continue your deep breathing and concentrate on the whirlpool of energy at the crown of your head. Remember that this Chakra never closes and needs to be sped up.

- Vividly imagine the spiritual whirlpool start to vibrate faster and spin faster. Your Crown Chakra is now opening further.

- Now imagine a brilliant ball of white energy hovering above your head. The white is so brilliant that it is difficult to look at it.

- Really feel the colour. Vividly create it in your mind. Now imagine the brilliant white light come gushing in through your Crown and engulf the inside of your body in this brilliant white energy.

- Enjoy the giddy feeling this creates in you for as long as you are happy ☺.

Now we are open psychically but we must close the Chakras down when we are finished or feel uncomfortable. To do this I want you to imagine the Third-Eye Chakra spinning very fast like a whirl pool. I now want you to imagine the Chakra slowing down until it stops. Now imagine sealing this Chakra in a brilliant white light. This is now closed.

I now want you to imagine the Crown Chakra spinning very fast like a whirl pool. I now want you to imagine the Chakra slowing down. This Chakra doesn't close so we just want to slow it down. When you feel it is slow enough seal this Chakra in a brilliant white light. This Chakra is now back to normal.

Meditation

The secret of all spiritual work is knowing how to meditate properly. I am not saying that everyone who can meditate can communicate with the spirit world. However, anyone who feels that they would like to become more sensitive to the spirit world must first learn to meditate. When a medium tunes in to the spirit world around them they take themselves to that point were we are just about to fall asleep…The cusp between awake and sleep state. It never ceases to amaze me the amount of people who try to do any sort of spiritual work without meditating. They sit down still creased up with all of the stresses of their everyday life and expect to be able to pick up the delicate messages from spirit. It is like going to a job interview wearing nothing but your underwear… it is pointless and is destined to end in failure. ☺

The first thing we have to ask ourselves is what meditation technique suits me best? There are so many techniques out there and it can be quite daunting trying to choose the one that suits your needs. I have chosen a few techniques that I find useful for spirit work and I am sure that you will find one of these that will work perfectly for you.

Preparation for all meditations in this book

Find yourself a room where you feel comfortable and one where you will not be disturbed during your meditation session. You will need somewhere to sit such as a chair or maybe a nice comfortable bed. The main aim is to have a place where you can sit comfortably were you will not begin to ache after a few minutes. I can never understand the people who choose to sit on the floor with their legs crossed and meditate for hours. I have tried this and lasted about 3 minutes before getting cramp and having to fall over and roll about before I managed to free my legs from this agonising predicament ☺ However, as I always say everyone to their own ☺

Concentration Meditation

This is a technique that I have always used and to be honest I don't even remember where I first learned it. I may have read it in a book years ago or it may have been passed to me by another spiritual person.

Technique

Sit with your feet placed firmly on the floor and your back kept straight. I want you to now sit for five minutes listening to your breathing. Breathe in through your mouth thinking 'fresh' as you fill your body with the freshness of life and exhale through your nose thinking 'relaxing' as your release all the stress and tension from your body.

After about five minutes of 'breathing' I want you to now concentrate fully on your feet. I want you to feel your feet using nothing but your senses...feel the socks (if you are wearing any☺) against your feet... are they soft all over?

Soft at the top but rougher near the toe area...feel your shoes against your socks etc. The main thing is that your full concentration is focused on your feet. Now I want you to move your concentration up to your legs…do the same again… feel the trousers against your legs etc. Again full concentration is the secret. I want you to now carry on doing this concentration technique until you reach your head area, concentrating fully on each area. Now I want you to concentrate on your head area and this time I want you to really concentrate and feel your hair on your head (if you have some ☺ If not concentrate and feel your scalp☺). What you have now done is internally grounded yourself.

Now I want you to concentrate on the external world. I want you to concentrate on the room around you. I want you to concentrate fully on everything in the room… every sound …the temperature… the emotions of the room (does it make you feel sad, happy?) Rather than let the noises around you interrupt your meditation, let them enhance it. The reason I want you to concentrate so much on your surroundings as well as your inner self is it will help you sense when there is a change in your external world. If a spirit enters the room you will immediately feel the difference ☺

The Beyond The Ego Meditation (my own creation)

We must pay attention to the activities of the body, how our mind constantly changes (both emotionally and intelligently). We must learn what the reason behind them is. To be at one with the Universe we must first learn to be at one with our body. Too many people try to be at one with the Universe, with nature and so on without first learning to be at one with themselves. When I point it out that they are ignoring the most important part of the Universe… THEM… they suddenly feel as if they have been hit by a bolt of lightening. To me this is what spiritual teaching is all about.

I am now going to surprise many people by arguing that we shouldn't be thinking about their bodies as a spiritual thing they should be viewing them as mere physical vessels assigned to us for the journey through this physical plane. However, they should still be viewed with great awe as they are a miracle produced by the Greater energy (I will be talking more about this in my next book). The mind is different we must view the mind as a different energy from the physical body.

Even though the physical vessel (body) and our spirit (mind) are two separate entities sharing the same space they are linked with cause and effect. An example of this is:

Close your eyes and concentrate on your breathing for five minutes. Now I want you to think about a time in your life that you were very happy. Really concentrate on this memory… feel the emotions, the colours, where are you? Who is with you? What has happened? And so on.

Slowly open your eyes… how does your body feel? Do you feel how light your body feels? How you feel as if you are excited about something… butterflies in your tummy… YOUR spirit (mind) has caused this change in your body… However, think how your spirit (mind) feels now… excited thoughts… happy thoughts… confident thoughts. So your body relaxing with the aid of your mind has in turn caused your mind to receive a positive energy boost…all in the space of minutes. You are now beginning to see just how powerful a tool your spirit (mind) is. Now you can see why we tend to pick up more illnesses etc when we are feeling low. When things are going bad in our life we almost always catch every virus and bug going around. When we are feeling positive and everything is going great in our life we tend to pick up very few viruses and bugs.

Spirit (mind) must not be confused with the ego. In order to understand this statement I must first make clear what I mean when I talk about the ego. When we are born onto this plane we have no ego… when we move onto the next plane we have no ego. The 'healthy' ego is formed when other people start to tell us nice things about ourselves. This energy builds the more we are told nice things. A healthy ego will help to energise the spirit (mind) and in turn the spirit will energise the body. However, what happens if people don't tell us nice things? What happens if we grow up in a world were people tell us that we are worthless and no good and always bringing us down no matter what we try to do? This has the opposite effect and an 'unhealthy' ego is formed. Instead of energising the body and the mind this energy sucks energy from the body and mind. We end up with mental illnesses such as depression. If this happens it makes sense to attempt to making the ego healthy rather than trying to cure the depression. (I will discuss this further in my next book). So another way of looking at the ego is that it is like a spiritual tape recorder... it records other people vocalised thoughts and opinions of us and uses them to affect our body and spirit (mind). So we can now see that the physical vessel (body), spirit (mind) and the ego are actually three separate entities sharing the same space.

This is why I feel that we must make sure our actions are pure and with the noblest intentions. If your actions aren't pure and you do things at the expense of other peoples happiness or you try and con people then you will be punished by your own ego. If you are caught, people will say horrible things to you about your deed and this will be recorded by the energy known as your ego. Your ego will then go from a 'healthy' ego to an 'unhealthy' ego and turn on your body and spirit. In my beliefs this is part of Karma.

Technique

Sit with your feet placed firmly on the floor and your back kept straight. I want you to now sit for five minutes listening to your breathing. Breathe in through your mouth thinking 'fresh' as you fill your body with the freshness of life and exhale through your nose thinking 'relaxing' as your release all the stress and tension from your body.

I now want you examine your body using your spirit (mind). Think about it as a separate entity from your spirit and ego as we discussed. Watch it as if you are watching someone else's body. Feel how it breathes, twitches, heart beats and so on. Let it amaze you as it works all on its own. This wonderful miracle of the

Greater Energy is existing on its own without requiring our spirit (mind) to work it. It will continue to do so until it is time for our spirit to be set free and move onto the next plane.

It is now time to examine the ego... how do we do this? I hear you cry! Psychologists have tried for years to finally crack the ego and all its mysteries so how can we do it in one meditation session? The answer very simply is that we won't. We aren't going to try and crack the secrets all we want to do is observe it. To do this we have to now concentrate on our spirit (mind). Now that we have observed our body as a separate entity we can now feel the spirit just 'existing' inside this vessel. Feel the power of the energy as it interlinks with all other energies around it (including spirit energy already set free from their vessels (known as the dead by our society). Again I will be looking at this more in-depth in my next book. You can now feel that you are at one with the universe. Simply an energy co-existing and intermingling with other energies. What thoughts enter your head as you sit in awe at this sensational energy? Don't try and answer the questions as they are being asked by the ego. Simply observe the questions… listen to the words but look for the meaning behind them. Does the ego blame everyone else for the bad things that happen and you for the good things that happen? Or does it have the opposite behaviour? Does it credit the world around you for the good things and chastise you for the bad things that happen? The 'healthy' ego will do the first and the 'unhealthy' ego will do the latter. For now the aim is just to watch all three entities interacting with each other. This helps us to meditate and relax and also see the world in a different way. In my next book we will look at how we can use this to help make an 'unhealthy' ego 'healthy' and in turn make an unhappy life happy.

Musical Meditation (My own creation)

Using music to meditate to is nothing new and has been used for this purpose for many years. However, from my experience music is used as a peaceful background for meditation rather than be the focus of meditation. In this technique I'm about to show you music can be used as the actual meditation. No matter what kind of music turns you on, whether it be classical, light rock, eighties music, sixties music… or even heavy metal, it can be used as the focus of meditation.

Technique

To start with I want you to find a recording of your most favourite piece of music in the world. I don't care what it is or what style of music it is. The important thing is that it is a piece of music that you love. The reason for this is that this piece of music will stir positive emotions in you. My favourite piece is 'marooned' by the wonderful Pink Floyd. Switch it on and set it to repeat so that it will restart without you losing your meditative state. I prefer to use my earphones so as to avoid Carole-Anne and the kids moaning at my taste in music being played loud ☺

Sit with your feet placed firmly on the floor and your back kept straight. I want you to now sit for five minutes listening to your breathing. Breathe in through your mouth thinking 'fresh' as you fill your body with the freshness of life and exhale through your nose thinking 'relaxing' as your release all the stress and tension from your body.

Now I want you to not just listen to the music but enter the music. Carefully listen to the lyrics and meditate on why the artist wrote those words…what is the message behind them…love? Sadness? Really let those words go through your subconscious and see what images they conjure and what journey they take you on. Really concentrate on the music… the different notes, tempo, and the tune…everything about the music and again see what images the music conjures up. I want you to know this piece of music inside out after a few sessions. This isn't just about the music though. We are using the music as a means to conjure up those images and thoughts. What we want to do is observe the images and thoughts without questioning or interfering with them. These images and thoughts are our subconscious and this is a way of tapping into it.

Next I want you to take one of the images and continue to meditate whilst allowing this image to go around in your head. What thoughts and feelings are you now experiencing? These thoughts and feelings are messages for you from your unconscious mind.

Now I want you to slowly remember where you are and begin to open your eyes. Quickly write down the thoughts, feelings and any messages you have been given whilst meditating. The likelihood is you will have been tapping into your subconscious…however, the more you do this the deeper your relaxed state will become and the closer you will be to reaching the state I achieve whilst communicating with spirit…thus, the more you do this the more chance you will have of receiving messages from spirit as well as your subconscious mind. I can hear you asking me how I know the difference between thoughts from my unconscious mind and messages from the spirit world. The answer to this is that only you can answer that but I can help you find the answer to it. The difference between our normal thought process and spirit communication can be very subtle. However, once we get too used to spirit communication we can tell the difference immediately. Does the same image keep coming to you whilst in meditation? If so what emotions do you feel when you visualise it? Do you feel happy? Sad? Frightened? tearful? Do any faces pop into your mind whilst meditating on this image? If so do you know this person? Do any words or sentences crop up whilst meditating on this image? This may all seem rather confusing, jumbled up and strange… welcome to the world of mediumship. What I want you to do now is see what link there is between the image, person, sentence etc. At this stage in your development I'd advise you to get yourself a pen and paper and write them down and look for the link. Through time this will come natural to you. It may turn out that this is a message you are getting for the persons whose face you saw. If this is the case always ask spirit to show themselves to you. This will come through in the same way as you saw the person you knows image. This means you will have a description of the spirit giving the message. Have they given you a name? Try asking them for a name? If so then wonderful as this allows you to go seek verification for the wonderful spiritual work you have done so far.

Obviously as a word of warning be careful how you bring this subject up as it may be from someone they have recently lost and may be very raw. Also only approach them for verification if you know them personally. Never approach them if the message you have received is of a negative nature as this goes against everything that I hold dear to me as spiritualism. Through time you can ask for more information from the spirit for verification. It is always nice when they give you some piece of information that you could possibly never know.

Certain people who are well developed in the art of mediumship, such as myself, can hear this thought process as a voice and also very clear images very much like a photograph. I am not telling this to dishearten you more to inspire you. It lets you know that if you persevere and work hard (because it will be hard work) in time you will begin to bring through much clearer messages and images. You will eventually, if gifted enough, begin to bring through messages for other people from friends and family from the spirit world on a regular basis. This is the first step in realising any mediumship gifts that you have and will help you know exactly what you are looking for when you finally take your new learned skills to your paranormal investigation.

Scientific Paranormal Investigation Tools

In this section I'm going to have a look at the scientific gadgets used by professional paranormal investigators and give a brief description of what the gadget is and what its function is. We have all seen them on television or on Ghost hunts but even though many people know what they are they don't know what they are for.

Anemometers & Velocity

Description: A device used for measuring wind speed or velocity.

Paranormal Use: This could be used to find out if there are any drafts coming in from any other sources that can then be used to explain cold spots etc.

Digital Thermometers

Description: The more modern versions of these are a bit like a gun. You basically point the instrument and a little red dot will show up. Aim this where you want to get a reading and press the trigger.

Paranormal Use: This is good for finding the different temperatures in various points of the room. If someone starts to feel hot or cold the gadget man can point the thermometer near them and measure them very quickly.

EMF Meters

Description: A gadget that measures Electromagnetic Fields. You've all seen them on television I'm sure. They are the little gadgets with the high pitched scream.

Paranormal Use: It is claimed that spirits emit Electromagnetic Force. However, many scientists rubbish this claim and question why paranormal Investigators bother with them for hunting ghosts.

EVP Sound Recorders

Description: EVP stands for Electronic Voice Phenomena. Basically they are unexplained noises heard on a recording machine. These machines apparently pick up messages from spirit.

Paranormal Use: The Investigator will record him/herself asking questions and then will stay silent for about 15 seconds. On playing the recording back they will listen for any unusual sounds on the machine. This will be electronically manipulated to try and hear if it forms a word.

Motion Detectors

Description: These are like little alarm systems that are activated when anything moves in the area being measured.

Paranormal Use: These gadgets can be set up in areas with high rates of reported paranormal phenomena.

When the group are away from that area then they will know if something or someone enters that area.

Spiritual Paranormal Investigation Tools

I don't think we can talk about Scientific Investigation Tools without now talking about what I like to call Spiritual Investigation Tools ☺. These are tools that parapsychologists will not class as paranormal evidence gaining and will argue that the effects are nothing more than psychological. I personally think this is an easy escape route for them ☺. I will also give instructions on how to make your own equipment ☺ See you can do this ghost hunting lark on the cheap after all ☺

Ouija Boards

Ouija (pronounced WEE-JA) Boards have got such a bad press in the past couple of decades. We've all heard the ghost stories from friends who claim to have had a bad experience with an evil entity on a Ouija board. I remember my friend telling me when we were teenagers that he had used a board whilst on a holiday with his friends. The story goes that they got in contact with an evil spirit that brought through lots of evil stuff and told them that one of them was going to die etc. It apparently ended with the glass being thrown from the board and smashing into thousands of little pieces. They then took the board (well pieces of paper that they had written letters on) and burnt it with all of the pieces of glass. They swore to me that they would never use a Ouija Board again as they were *"Pure Evil"*.

However, as long as a medium is present and the board is opened and closed properly then there won't be any problems. A medium can remove any darker entities who decide to use the board.

Building your own Ouija Board

You will need

- A smooth piece of wood to use as your Ouija Board. I find a good cheap material for this is MDF as it is smooth and has no grain to interrupt the movement of the glass. The size of this is totally up to your self. As long as it has the room for the writing then it is big enough. Make sure it isn't too big to comfortably reach the centre of the board.

- A pencil.

- Black and other colours of paint for designing your board.

- A fine paintbrush.

- A glass or Planchette.

Method

1. If you are using MDF then you are ready to start designing your board. If you are using wood then sand the board until it is completely smooth and easy for the glass to move without effort. I'd recommend an electric sander for this job.

2. using your pencil mark the outline of the words 'YES' 'NO' and 'GOODBYE' in the centre of 3 of the outer edges of the board. Now take your pencil and mark the outline of the letters of the alphabet around the outer edges of the board.

3. Take your paint brush and fill in the letters and words in black paint. Take your time doing this part as this will be your board for a long time to come and people will be paying very close attention to it whilst using it.

4. Now is the fun part in my opinion and also the part that makes your board personal to you. Using other people's boards is all very well but there is something very special about using a board that

you have designed and put your energy into. Take your paint brush and paint any designs and colours that your intuition makes you feel that you want to.

5. (This part is optional). Many people like to varnish the board to protect the artwork that is now on it. Personally I don't like to do this as I feel it blocks the energy. I prefer allowing it to age naturally and if needed be touched up again (it can be argued that this will allow you to add more energy to it).

Spiritual Protection of the Board

Many theories exist as to what kind of protection one needs when using a Ouija Board. I have heard theories ranging from blood on the newly created board to doing some sort of ritualistic dance round it whilst calling out the names of Pagan Gods etc. I personally use the following method to protect any new board that I create:

- Stand beside your new Ouija Board looking down on it.

- Imagine a ball of brilliant white light above you hovering. This brilliant white light is the energy of protection.

- I now want you to imagine this light coming down over your board and engulfing the board in the bright white light of protection.

- Now say the following prayer:

"With the power of my spirit guides and relatives now existing on the higher planes this board is protected from all negative spirit energies."

How to use the Ouija Board

Opening the Ouija Board

Everyone should hold hands and imagine a ball of brilliant white energy hovering above the group. Now imagine this white light coming down onto the group and enveloping the group. This is the brilliant white light of protection and will keep the groups safe throughout the session. Relax whilst reciting a prayer or some nice words. There are many prayers and ceremonies for opening a Ouija Board properly. I like this one that appeared in the 'The Spirit Speaks' which was a weekly magazine/newspaper at the turn of the twentieth century.

"There is a land where we all go,

Whence ne'er the frost nor cold wind blow,

And friends remembered reunite,

And those who hate, forget their spite,

In glow surround these gentle beings,

We call you now to bless our meetings,

Heaven's promise, our spirits thrive,

So now for the Living, Let the dead come alive,

Greetings spirits, speak thee to us!

Conducting the Ouija Board Session

- Everyone place their finger on the glass or Planchette.

- The medium or chosen person to be the medium should now ask for all the spirits in the room to come forward to the table and move the glass to show their presence (this may take some time so be patient).

- Once the glass starts moving ask some questions. My advice is to start the session with yes or no answers until the energy builds up.

- Once the energy has built up you will notice that the glass will start to move very quickly and now more detailed questions can be asked of the spirit.

Closing the Ouija Board

This part is so simple yet so many people don't do it and leave the board open and prone to spirit activity carrying on after the session. Close the board as follows:

- Thank the spirits for communicating with you in a very respectable way.

- Move the glass or Planchette over the Goodbye.

- Everyone should now remove their fingers from the glass or Planchette.

Dowsing

This is an ancient technique whereby the 'Dowser' uses rods or pendulums to gain information about a subject or the whereabouts of an object, person or place. They can also be used to communicate with spirit by asking questions that require 'yes' or 'no' answers. This can be done by watching the rods or pendulums for a movement in a particular way. This will become clearer when I give you instructions on how to use them.

The dowsing tools themselves are not magical items (no matter what some people claim) thus can be made very inexpensively. They are merely tapping into the dowsers' subconscious mind and intuitive sensitivities. Thus, if they are being used to contact the spirit world then my beliefs are it is the person using the tools that is making the contact. The rods or pendulums are merely bringing that communication from out with the subconscious mind.

Making Your Own Dowsing Rods

You Will Need

- 2 pieces of copper wire or even ordinary wire (about 20" in length).

- Good strong tape.

- Sponge or tissue.

Method

1. Gently bend one end of the wire (about 5" from the end) until it makes a handle (a bit like the handle of an old cowboy gun).

2. Wrap the sponge (or tissue) around the handle you have just created and use the tape to secure it. This gives you a comfy handle to hold.

YOUR DOWSING RODS ARE NOW READY FOR USE! NOW HOW EASY WAS THAT ☺

How to Use the Dowsing Rods

- Take a rod in each hand.

- Gently hold the rod in your hand (see photograph below). The more relaxed you are and the less tightly you hold the rods then the more chance there is of the rods working for you.

- Hold your hands as if holding a gun about shoulder width apart.

- Hold the rods horizontally and make sure they are completely straight or they wont work. To prove this to your self hold them slightly up or slightly down and move them at will. Now try this whilst they are horizontal and straight. Can you see how much easier they move?

- Keep moving them at will whilst in this position until you get used to them.

- Now I want you to stop moving them at will. I want you to let them gently sit in the starting position (some people call this the neutral position as when they are asking a question and the rods go here it means the spirit is neutral to the question or maybe doesn't understand or want to answer the question.

- Ask spirit to move the rods to the right and watch the rods waiting for them to move. Be patient as this may take a while at first.

- Now ask spirit to move the rods back to the centre.

- Now ask spirit to move the rods to the left.

- Now ask spirit to move them back to the centre.

- Now finally ask spirit to cross the rods over each other.

- Now ask spirit to move them back to the centre.

Using Dowsing Rods in a Paranormal Investigation

Now that you are familiar with your rods they can be used during your paranormal investigation. After meditating I want to take your dowsing rods and tell them out loud that you want them to lead you to the spiritually active areas of the building. Slowly walk around the location letting the rods use your natural sensitivities. At all times keep in your mind what you are searching for and try not to let your mind wander off in another direction. Are the rods pointing you in a certain direction? Do they cross when you find a spiritually active area? Only you will be able to answer these questions when you finally get the opportunity to test them out for yourself. Now is this not a lot more satisfying than walking around a location letting the medium tell you what to feel and when to be scared etc. Hold on I'm doing myself out of a job ☺. Before I have every medium getting in touch with me to give me abuse I'd just like to make clear that I am not for one second suggesting that mediums are not needed on investigations. I am merely suggesting that we should be there for an initial walk around of the building and then be there in an advisory and guidance roll. Let people feel the wonderfully satisfying feeling of finding something that can be verified ☺.

Pendulums

Pendulums are the same idea as dowsing rods. They do exactly the same job and can be used for exactly the same purposes. The reason I am talking about them here is the fact that some people prefer to work with pendulums rather than rods.

Making Your Own Pendulums

Pendulums can be purchased from stores or online shops for as much as you are willing to pay for them. They can be absolutely beautiful items. They are normally made from crystal and encased in a pretty metal and held with a pretty chain. These are wonderful to look at and they really do look mysterious and professional. However, I'd just like to say that when pendulums were first used do you think they would have had access to all of this finery? The answer to this question wont surprise you... it is no. They would have used any object that was at hand. Like I mentioned earlier in the book it is not the dowsing tool that is magical it is you. So anything can be used as a pendulum. I have used everything from pebbles, pieces of wood I've carved, sink washers and so on. Here I am going to use one of the pieces from a wind chime. The reason I like to use these is the fact that they already have a hole drilled in them for the thread to be tied to. Trust me this saves a lot of hassle in the long run ☺ Wind chimes are made from many different materials and are always pretty so this gives you so much scope to choose from. The only thing I will say though is not to choose the wind chimes with long chimes on them as they would be too difficult to work with. I have chosen one that looks like the kind of diamond shapes you would find on a chandelier. These can be found very cheaply in stores such as IKEA etc.

You Will Need

- A piece from a wind chime (see the picture).

- A piece of fine string or a nice chain.

Method

1. Cut a piece of string or buy a nice chain (about 10 inches in length).

2. Feed your string (or chain) through the hole in your item and tie it in a knot.

You have just saved yourself a lot of money and now have a perfectly workable pendulum in your hand ☺

How to use your pendulum

- Find yourself somewhere that you are comfortable and relax.

- Take your string (or chain) between your thumb and first finger. It doesn't matter what hand you use…I tend to swap it between hands as I get tired.

- Move your hand about 10-14 inches away from your body.

- Stop the pendulum moving with your free hand and relax by concentrating on your breathing.

- Now ask spirit to move the pendulum for you. It doesn't matter which way this happens. It will usually be in a circle (either clockwise or anti-clockwise), back and forward or side to side.

- Once this happens ask spirit to stop the pendulum moving.

- Now ask spirit to show you what movement means yes.

- And now you want spirit to show you what movement means no.

- Now that you know this you need to find out what movement means neutral.

- You are now ready to ask spirit some questions. Obviously make sure that the questions you ask can be answered with a yes or no answer. This may seem an insult to your intelligence but it would amaze you the amount of questions I have heard asked that couldn't possibly be answered with a yes or no answer ☺

Automatic Writing Planchette

Believe it or not this is actually the original Ouija Board. It was invented as a means to communicate with the spirit world. The theory was that spirit would use the pen to write messages to the people using the Planchette. However, it was quickly realised that the response from spirit was very disjointed and the letters and words were very difficult to read. So someone came up with the idea of placing ready made letters under the Planchette and thus the Ouija Board was born.

Building your own Automatic Writing Planchette

You will need

- A small smooth piece of wood or a small piece of MDF.

- 4 small wheels (available from any DIY store).

- A drill.

- A pen.

- 2 clips to hold the pen in place.

- Sandpaper.

Method

1. Using sandpaper smooth the edges and corners of the MDF or wood.

2. Drill a hole on one end of the wood a few inches from end large enough to fit a pen into. If you get this perfect you won't need to fit the clips as it will jam the pen in and you will only have to replace the inner re-fill when the ink runs out.

3. Screw the small wheels to the bottom of the Planchette.

Using the Automatic Writing Planchette

- Place the Planchette on a large sheet of paper.

- Everyone gather round the Planchette and hold hands. Repeat the opening of the Ouija Board (as described earlier in this book.

- Everyone should place a finger on the Planchette.

- The medium (or the person at the table chosen to be the medium) should ask for the spirits in the room to come toward the table and move the Planchette as a sign of their presence.

- Again like the Ouija board this may take some time to happen so patience is required.

- When the Planchette begins to move ask the spirit to show you a sign for 'no' and a sign for 'yes'.

- Once this has been established the participants can begin to ask questions requiring yes and no answers.

- It can be quite nice to ask the spirit to draw you something as this can produce a message without yes or no questions and may lead your line of questioning in a totally different direction.

Closing Down the Planchette

Thank the spirits for all of their help and answers and say goodbye to the spirits. There is no 'goodbye' to point the Planchette at so each person must take turns in saying thank you and goodbye and then lifting their finger off. Continue round the group until there are no fingers left on the Planchette.

Psychometry

Psychometry is when the medium tunes into the energy of both an object and also the energies of those who have come into contact with the object. I don't have the room in a book about spiritual paranormal investigating to go into how energies affect objects but will be discussing this in my next book.

This, however, is more complicated than it sounds. Consider for a moment how many people will come into contact over the years with say a kitchen knife. If this kitchen knife was used in a murder and someone asked the medium to tune into the energies to see what they could find out about either the murderer or the victim what do you think would happen? You may be sitting thinking wow what a great idea for an experiment on a ghost hunting TV show. However, if you think about it for a second you will realise that maybe a dozen different people will have used the knife on regular occasions. The murderer may have used it once (stole it from a house for example) and the victim never at all. Who then do you think the information you receive will be about? The likelihood is it will be about the family and friends who used this knife and whose house it sat in. When the experimenter looked over the information he may decide that the medium has failed his test as the people described were nothing like the murderer or his victim. So don't class your self as a failure if the information you pick up does not match the information about the main person associated with that location as there will have been hundreds of people living there over the years.

The reason I am bringing Psychometry into this book is that I feel that it allows us to tune into all the energies associated with items of furniture and even the fabric of the walls. So rather than just thinking a room feels creepy you can try and find out some of the reasons why. Believe it or not sometimes the paranormal activity comes from the furniture rather than the location.

Before we attempt Psychometry it is advisable to open the small Chakras we have in the palm of our hands and the tips of our fingers. This will make any attempt at Psychometry so much more successful. This is done in a totally different way to the Chakra opening I taught you earlier in this book.

Simply rub your hands together as fast as you can. You will notice the palms of your hands becoming extremely hot. Now place one set of finger tips on the other set and rub them together briskly for a couple of minutes. You have now opened up the Chakras and are almost ready to begin Psychometry.

Now that your hands are ready it is time to focus your mind. There are many ways to do this but the one I like is the letters focusing schedule. This is as follows:

- Close your eyes and imagine the letter 'A' in front of you.

- Focus fully on this letter. Put everything else out of your mind and really concentrate on the letter 'A'.

- Once you have done this move on to the letter 'B'. Focus on this letter now. You should no longer have the letter 'A' in your thought process.

- Continue to do this until you feel fully focused.

Your mind is now focused and your hands are ready for Psychometry.

Method

- Close your eyes and concentrate on your breathing.

- Imagine your hands are surrounded by energy. It is going through them and around them. This psychic energy will enable them to tune into the energies of the object.

- Now imagine the energy engulfing and surrounding your whole body.

- Now open your eyes and take the object in your hands if possible. If it is too large then simply run your hands over it.

- As soon as anything comes to your mind say it out loud.

- What emotions are you feeling?

- Are any images or thoughts suddenly entering your mind?

This can be a wonderful way of finding new information about your location. It can also be a fun skill to learn for everyday life. Try it with your friends and family. Ask them to pass you objects and see if you can bring through specific details about the owner.

<u>Scrying</u>

The art of Scrying has been around for hundreds of years spanning many civilisations and cultures. Many objects have been used from the crystal ball to ink to water to mirrors. Very much like dowsing it is not the object that holds any psychic powers it is the individual using them.

Over the years there have been many famous scryers, but the one I'll mention here is the one that everyone has heard of. This is of course Nostradamus the 16th Century prophet who used Scrying to get his information about future events.

I will be using the same method in this book as Nostradamus used all those years ago. This is simply water in a bowl and meditation.

You will need

- A small bowl.

- Water.

- A candle.

- A table to sit at.

Method

1. Place your bowl on a dark surface if possible.

2. Fill the bowl with water (not too near the top or it'll make a mess ☺).

3. Light a candle and place it near enough to light up the water but not too close to set your hair on fire ☺). Be careful that nothing is reflecting onto the surface of the water.

4. Sit in front of your bowl of water and make sure you are comfortable.

5. Close your eyes and carry out the grounding part of the concentration meditation I taught you earlier in this book.

6. When you are ready open your eyes.

7. Carry out the same protection ceremony as for the Ouija Board.

8. Now I want you to look into the water and continue to imagine the white light washing over you and through the water.

9. You may eventually get bored but don't give up…just continue to concentrate on your breathing and the white light of protection.

10. If you see any visions in the water… fantastic ☺…If not then better luck next time as it doesn't always happen ☺.

On the Paranormal Investigation

Meditation

The first thing I'd advise anyone to do on arrival at the location is to find a nice quiet place and meditate. Choose one of the meditations I have shown you and carry this out. There are two reasons for this: firstly it allows you get your self into a nice relaxed state and helps you be at one with the energy of the building. Secondly it allows you to see if you immediately begin to get any re-occurring images, thoughts etc from the people who once lived in the location you are investigating. Imagine how excited you will be if after meditating you find that one of the images you have received once lived there and possibly even a painting of them exists or maybe something with their name on it. This would again be fantastic affirmation for you and if this happens then well done ☺.

The only problem when this happens is it leaves you open to accusations of fraud. Some people may say that you read the plaque or seen the painting before hand. My advice on dealing with this is to ignore them as they are not worth being allowed to destroy any good energy you have worked so hard to build up.

I can give you this advice as it happened to me very publicly by a certain individual (I will call Mr Toe-tap to keep his anonymity) who really should have known better. I was accused of taking a name from a wall in Lincoln Castle and using it in part of my communication with spirit. However, this person was so fraudulent that he never challenged me about it until I left his group. He allowed me to carry on with my communication AND was actually affected with this name as the night went on. At one point I saw him running about in apparent fear claiming to anyone who would listen that he heard him whisper in his ear and so much more. So in this case I would ask you who was more fraudulent? Was it me for getting through the same name that appeared on a wall in part of the Castle (however, I would argue that if this name is on a wall somewhere in the castle and I am communicating with spirit who once spent time in this castle then surely it would make sense that possibly this spirit would indeed have communicated with me. It would have made a more compelling argument if this person had never existed in the first place) or was it the person who had this doubt and chose to go along with it and even pretend to be affected by it until I had walked away from his group? This will happen to many mediums over the coming months, years and decades. We are the easy target for anyone who wants to rubbish paranormal occurrences in locations. However, it is the way you deal with this that matters. Keep your head held high and know that you are working truthfully for spirit and you'll never go wrong. Anyone who is knowingly working fraudulently and claiming it to be the spirit world will be dealt with by Karma and when we finally finish our work on this plane.

Your Initial Walk around on your own

After meditating go for a walk around the location to feel the different energies in the various rooms and to allow yourself to see if anymore messages enter your mind whilst doing so. Fight the temptation to do this in tourist mode though, as you are here tapping into energies not to look at the fine arts etc that may be on display. Walk into each room and stand quietly in the middle with your eyes closed resuming your meditative state (this will become easier to do the more you practice). I want you to now feel the energy of the room. Are you feeling any emotions? Are any images being brought to your attention? Are any name coming into your head? Are any dates coming through? Through time they may even begin to replay events for you, such as showing you the building on fire or someone being hanged or maybe someone falling from a window and so on. By now you should be starting to get the idea of how a medium can walkabout bringing through so much information. I go through this process at EVERY location I investigate. As you learned when we spoke about meditation this process is very complicated at times and has to be made sense of us firstly by us before we pass that information on to others.

Paranormal Experiments

Throughout the night I want you to use the different techniques that I have taught you in this book. Decide at the beginning of the evening where and when you will use each technique. If it feels suitable then feel free to use one or more of the techniques at several parts of the location. Basically it's your investigation and all I've done is furnish you with the necessary skills and knowledge to undertake a paranormal investigation.

The Séance

I think the best way to start this section is by answering the question, *"What is a séance?"*

"My definition of a séance is: A group of concurring individuals assembled in a controlled setting to participate in a spiritual experiment led by a medium."

In other words a group of people gathered together to try and communicate with the spirit world through a medium. Other methods will be used to try and aid communication by all participants. The medium is there as the link between this plane and the higher planes. He/she will pass on messages that spirit want the group (or individuals within the group) to hear.

Preparation

- Choose between 6-8 people to participate in the séance.

- If there are sceptics present in the room ensure they are there as open-minded observers rather than participants. The reason for this is scepticism can interfere with the flow of spiritual energy.

- Find a table large enough to fit everyone around.

- Make sure you know what you want from spirit. In other words what questions you have etc.

Method

1. Everyone in the group hold hands and close your eyes.

2. I want everyone to relax and think about what you want to happen from the session and the evening as a whole.

3. The medium should now move round the group ensuring that everyone is doing their breathing exercises properly.

4. I now want everyone to put their hands on the table (palms down) and have your little fingers touching the little fingers of the people on either side of you.

5. Relax and concentrate on your breathing. Breathe in through your mouth and out through your nose.

6. Now I want you to imagine a ball of brilliant white light hovering above the group.

7. Everyone say together, *"This is the white light of protection."*

8. I want you to really conjure up this image in your minds eye.

9. I now want you to imagine this brilliant white light moving down onto your heads. This light moves all the way down your bodies before enveloping the group.

10. Everyone say together, *"This is the white light of protection."*

11. You are now protected throughout the session.

12. The medium should now ask, *"All spirits in this room please come forward to this circle. Pass messages through our third eye or affect someone in the group. We are here with the greatest respect no matter our beliefs."*

13. This may take a few attempts before anything begins to happen…be patient.

14. Once activity does begin to happen always respectfully say, *"Thank-you"*.

15. Things that may happen are: Vivid Images placed in the groups mind using the third-eye, thoughts placed using the third-eye, delicate touching like a cobweb brushing against your face, the feeling of someone gently pushing you backwards or forwards or both, your hair may be gently touched.

16. At the end the séance I want you to say, "*We thank you for everything you have done for us. It is now time for us to end this communication.*"

17. The group should now take turns at saying thank-you.

A Few Of My Paranormal Investigations

Berkeley Castle

Historical Background

This wonderful Castle was originally built as a Norman fortress and has been residence to the Berkeley family for over 900 years. After filming for a television show there

I was told that the Castle is the oldest building in the country to be inhabited by the same family who built it. The thought of ONE family living in the same building for 900 years blows my mind. The Castle was originally built to keep out the invading Welsh and much evidence of this past life can still be seen there today. It is a place that has many stories linked to it. It has even been witness to the Royal murder of Edward II in 1327!

During its life-time the Castle has collected, and still contains, many historical items. These include Francis Drake's cabin chest, Queen Elizabeth I's bedspread, and the banner that the 4th Earl of Berkeley took with him to the Battle of Culloden. As well as these historical treasures the castle includes many beautiful paintings and wonderful tapestries.

However, what amazed me most on entering this Castle was how beautiful it was. Inside is a courtyard that is absolutely stunning and wouldn't be out of place in a Disney film. It is so stunning that one would be forgiven for assuming that this place could never be haunted.

However, when the sun goes down and the lights go off the beauty becomes the beast. I'd recommend this fantastic place for people with an interest in the paranormal AND people with a love of history or architecture.

Paranormal stories linked to Berkeley Castle

The scream of the murdered King Edward II

It is rumoured that King Edward II was killed when a red hot poker was thrust up his rectum. I don't know about you, the reader, but to me this sounds like one of the most painful forms of torture one could endure. Imagine being killed in such a gruesome and degrading way. The story goes that when the King was tortured and murdered in this way his scream was so loud and frightening that it could be heard as far away as the town of Berkeley. However, having investigated the castle I personally feel that the distance would make this part of the story very unlikely. One of the most common paranormal phenomena reported there is the blood curdling scream of the poor King echoing round the Castle corridors and local vicinity.

The funeral procession

It was reported that a group of young people from the nearby town of Berkeley were walking home, as they had done many previous evenings before, from the pub. On their journey home they passed the castle, and didn't give it a second glance. However, suddenly a door opening caught their eye and from the door emerged a ghostly horse drawn funeral procession. The procession was led by a ghostly monk and remained for a few seconds before disappearing into the night air. Was this vision down to too much beer or was it indeed a replay of the murdered Kings funeral?

The phantom piano

The piano that sits in the Great Hall has been heard to play on its own. Is this a phantom music lover or something more sinister?

Berkeley Castle through the eyes of a medium

The Morning Room

On walking into this pretty little room with tapestries around and comfortable furniture I was overcome with the feeling of holiness. People will ask, rightly so, How can you describe the feeling of being holy? The answer to that is that it is a feeling of being completely good but at the same time slightly frustrated. I always get the feeling that I have to work very hard at being good and that this goodness is someone else's definition of the word. Almost as if I am being ordered to feel the way I feel and do the things I do. This is in no way a criticism of anyone who considers themselves holy. It is more the way that I feel when this feeling overcomes me.

Here the energy I was picking up was residual energy rather than actual intelligent spiritual contact. From the residual energy I could feel the presence of a man. Again, I will explain how I came to this conclusion. When working with residual energy I conclude the gender by the feeling in the energy. A male presence tends to feel much heavier and more aggressive than a female energy. The female energy has a more airy feeling to it and almost feels quite sweet. With the earlier feeling of holiness I came to the conclusion that this spirit was a man of the cloth. I will now contradict my earlier statement by admitting that I was now bringing through the feeling of sadness and anger. As my night in this location continued I discovered that the sadness and anger from this man was due to the fact that the Morning Room was and, in his opinion, still should be a chapel. He was angry that this chapel was being disrespected so much in its present day use and decor.

The Great Hall

The first thing that struck me on entering the Great Hall was the size of the place. This room was over sixty foot in length and over 40 foot in width! The hall was absolutely beautiful with rich tapestries on the wall and marble all around me.

The first spirit that contacted me was a man who came across as quite a character indeed. Whilst communicating with me he tried very hard to make me laugh. He reminded me of a little boy who was desperate to be centre of attention. The image that was put into my head was that of a joker from a packet of playing cards (without the funny hat). However, I picked up a tragic feeling whilst speaking to this man. After composing myself for a few minutes I began to get the feeling that this poor man had lost his life in that very room. I suddenly had the feeling that I was falling. Anytime I have had this in the past it has almost always turned out to be the cause of death. The tragic thing for me was that shortly after experiencing this feeling I was told by the spirit that he was pushed from the balcony above.

The Kings Gallery

The thing that struck me about this area was that despite it being a very pleasant and comfortable place it felt to me like a prison. The reason I felt this about it was I had the feeling of being trapped, frustrated and hopeless. You may state that this could also mean that it was someone trapped here in an accident or some other situation. I agree that this is possible, however, in that kind of situation there is also the feeling of fear.

I now started to communicate with a male spirit who was, in my opinion Royalty. This comes through in the form of feeling better than everyone else and feeling that I am superior to everyone in the room. I almost feel as if I should gesture in some respectful way to the spirit. I also started to feel as if I wanted to run out of this area.

In this area was a semi circle with a banister around it and a small sign reading, 'Dungeon'. The banister was surrounding what can only be described as a drop of about 20 feet. I felt that this wasn't any ordinary dungeon as I was getting images of people being thrown down into this pit. This shocked me as I always have the idea of a dungeon being a room where people were taken to and chained up.

Small room off of The Kings Gallery

This room gave me the feeling of death. This feeling comes to me as a thick, dark feeling and is usually associated with murder. This is a different feeling from someone dying of natural causes. I was pretty sure that this death was the death of the earlier Royal figure. I was now convinced that this spirit was King Edward. He had a particular corner of the room that he didn't like people occupying the space. Now he started to tell me that he did not like my Scottish accent (how dare he ha ha). He started to confide in me that when he was on this plane that there was a lot of talk about him having relationships with other men. He was telling me that this was the reason he was tortured. However, he still argues that it was all lies, made up by those who would benefit from his death.

My lasting thoughts on Berkeley Castle

After spending a night in this magnificent Castle I am left with many different emotions. I feel empathy with the priest and would love to see the morning room transformed back into a chapel. I feel that this would allow this unhappy man rest in the knowledge that all is as it should be. I feel so much sympathy and sadness for the poor Joker (Jester) and the King for the tragic circumstances surrounding their deaths. However, what will stay with me is the beauty of the place. If you're going to haunt a Castle then I suppose it makes sense to pick one as pretty as Berkeley Castle.

Carlisle Castle

Historical Background

On the site of Carlisle Castle originally stood a wooden Roman Fort in the 1st to 4th centuries AD serving the western end of Hadrian's Wall, which by the time the Castle was built stood empty. The Castle was ordered to be built from timber; in an area that it is believed was part of Scotland at the time, during the reign of William II of England. However, William soon hounded the Scots from the area and re-claimed it for England once more. Now over 900 years later Carlisle Castle still stands proudly. Its main function was to keep out the invading Scottish armies. For this reason, and its position, it was the scene of many conflicts during its lifetime. In 1122 Henry I of England decided that it was time to build a stone Castle on the site, along with City walls. Over the following centuries the Castle changed hands between Scotland and England many times. In fact between the years 1306 and 1307 the Castle was also the seat of government to the English Parliament.

The most famous prisoner at Carlisle castle was Mary Queen of Scots between 18th May and 13th July 1568, 2 months after her abdication of the Scottish throne in 1568. However, the tower in which she was imprisoned in has since been demolished. During the English Civil war the Castle was occupied by the parliamentarian forces for eight months. In my opinion the most important occupation of the Castle was in 1745 when Bonnie Prince Charlie and his army seized it. During this time the Castle was controlled by the Jacobite army, only for the forces to be driven out of England once more, this time by the Duke of Cumberland's army. The Jacobite's were arrested and held in the dungeons and executed. In fact it is said by some that the beautiful Scottish ballad, 'Loch Lomond' was written in the dungeons by one of the Jacobite prisoners to his sweetheart in the Scottish Highlands.

Paranormal stories linked to Carlisle Castle

The Ghost of the unknown lady

Carlisle castle is said to be haunted by the ghost of an unknown lady. In the 1800's a soldier on guard is said to have saw her and called for her to halt. She kept going and the angry soldier tried to stab her with his bayonet... however, he went right through her and his blade got stuck in the wall behind her. The story goes that he collapsed and died of shock shortly afterwards. What makes this story more spooky and remarkable is the fact that in 1820 a woman's skeleton wearing a Scottish tartan and holding the skeleton of a small child was discovered bricked up in the Captain's Tower!

Ghostly soldiers, screams and the playful jester

Over the years there have been many sightings of all different kinds of soldiers in various parts of the Castle. Also many people have claimed to have heard the screaming of ghostly Jacobite soldiers held captive in the dungeons. It has been reported by various people over the years that they have had tricks played on them by the ghost of a mischievous jester.

The moaning dark figures

In the dungeon of the Castle many sightings have been reported of dark figures walking about the dungeons moaning as if in great pain. It has even been claimed that one of these dark figures actually attacks people in the dungeon area.

The shape shifter

Sightings of a shape shifter have been numerous over the years. For anyone who doesn't know, a shape shifter is a person or other being capable of changing their physical form. In other words someone who has the ability to change their physical appearance at will. In the keep there is a chair where varied accounts of a shape have been told. These vary from the shape of a man to other figures.

Carlisle Castle through the eyes of a medium

The Dungeon

On walking into this cold, damp depressing room I immediately felt uneasy. Straight away I was summoned over to the corner of the room by a male presence named Donald. This man was immediately recognisable as a Scotsman. He wore a white shirt and a green/blue kilt. He told me that he had been held prisoner in the dungeon after being captured in battle. They placed him and hundreds of his fellow soldiers in this small dungeon. He then started to tell me a story about how his captors were coming into the dungeon and randomly picking people to hang. However, he also mentioned that they were playing with the prisoner's emotions as they would then arrive and set someone free. One can only imagine how horrible this must have felt, hearing the door open and not knowing whether you wanted to be chosen or not. Have you been chosen to be hanged or have you been chosen to return to your family and friends. The one emotion that stayed with me all the way through this connection was fear.

Suddenly from nowhere he told me to touch a part of the wall that had been worn away. He continued to tell me that this part of the wall is what kept the men alive... the dampness...they would drink it!

The corridor outside the dungeon

I didn't communicate with any spirits here but on a few occasions I heard very loud footsteps when the corridor was empty!

A Store Room on the Second Floor

This room was bare with no carpets or furnishings. In this room waiting for me was a man in his late 50's/early 60's with a really big moustache. Apart from his moustache the distinct feature of this man was his huge frilly collar similar to the one worn by altar boys. Unfortunately I didn't get the opportunity to communicate with this man as he disappeared very quickly. However, later in the night this man returned to me and told me his names was Sir Francis N.... Unfortunately I didn't manage to make out his surname. He then told me he was here looking after a prisoner. This wasn't just any old prisoner but a Queen. He told me that he was teaching this Queen English and that she always asked to speak to Queen Elizabeth. It turned out that this was Mary Queen of Scots who was held in the Castle.

The Castle Keep

This room again was bare with no carpet or furnishings. Here I got the sense of soldiers preparing for some sort of battle. Again this is one of those moments were one may feel moved to ask how can you feel military? The feeling I get in this part of the process is one of great pride and excitement... I can feel the nerves and I start to get images of battles in my head. At this point the image of Donald flashed into my head and it became obvious to me that these were the same soldiers that were coming to get them to hang or let go.

Just as I was starting to get more information a female spirit dressed in a long flowing dress walked into the room, beckoned me and left. She did this quite a few times. I got the impression she was trying to get me to follow her. Unfortunately, at that point in time I didn't have the opportunity to follow her. I knew she didn't belong in that part of the castle. The reason I knew? The energy was different from the energy of that area of the castle. Each room I enter in any location has a certain energy. This energy comes from many things, such as the bricks, the spirits, the furniture and the general atmosphere. If any spirit not belonging to that room enters I instantly feel the change in the energy.

Later in the evening on entering the Castle Keep again I felt the presence of a more sinister spirit. This spirit refused to communicate with me and really freaked me out by making the other people with me, and I think we had seen each other in places we weren't. In other words I'd think I had seen X stand beside me... turn around and X would be in front of me. This has never happened to me before and it felt nice to be spooked for once! However, what I didn't like is I knew that this thing was pure evil!

My lasting thoughts on Carlisle Castle

Carlisle castle goes down as one of the very few places that have actually freaked me out. I would go as far as to say that I was spooked. I can still feel the fear of poor Donald as he waited for those horrible footsteps of the guards coming to get them to either hang them or set them free. I'm left with the disappointment that I didn't get the opportunity to follow the spirit of the lady to find out what she wanted to show me.

It still seems strange to me that the Queens jailer/protector was teaching her English and I am left with the feeling of desperation that Mary Queen of Scots had to see Queen Elizabeth. Poor lady must have been desperate to receive some sort of comforting news from her.

All in all I'd recommend Carlisle Castle to anyone interested in the Paranormal!

Kiplin Hall

Historical Background

Kiplin Hall was built in the 1620s for George Calvert, Secretary of State to James I. Mr Calvert later went on to become the 1st Lord Baltimore and founder of Maryland, USA. Kiplin Hall differs from other houses of this era due to the position and style of the towers. Instead of the normal corner towers there were domed towers on each side with a central pavilion. During its 4 centuries of existence the property has seen 4 families living there (all related by blood and marriage). These families were the Calvert's (17th Century), the Crowe's (18th Century), the Carpenter's (19th Century) and the Talbot's (part of the 20th Century).

Inside the Hall hosts a collection of paintings by Louisa, Marchioness of Waterford and, of a more chilling nature, a lump of wood that is rumoured to be part of the block on which Charles I lost his head. The other interesting piece of furniture is a library chair used by Admiral Nelson aboard the HMS Victory.

Paranormal stories linked to Kiplin Hall

There have been many paranormal sightings in this spooky building including, ghostly footsteps, and the strange sound of someone crying in a drawing room. There has been a female spirit spotted on the stair case and also a 1940's airman spotted in one of the kitchens. No haunted location would be complete without those spooky smells and Kiplin Hall doesn't disappoint. There have been smells of pipe tobacco and also the smell of a gentleman's cologne reported.

Female figure in upstairs service corridor

This corridor was opened to link two separate wings of the Hall for easy access by the servants. A lady has been seen walking up and down this corridor on many occasions. Is this lady a servant going about her business?

Lady in Drawing Room

In this beautiful drawing room the pitiful sight of a lady sitting at the window crying has been reported by many different visitors. Is this Lady one of the 4 families who have called this Hall home? Is she crying for her lost love or waiting for a family member to return from war?

Poltergeist Activity in a room off the Long Gallery

Whilst standing in the Long gallery many people have reported hearing banging from an adjoining room. Like most poltergeist activity nothing happens when anyone is actually in the room. Is this an unhappy child trying to attract people's attention?

Kiplin Hall through the eyes of a medium

The Library

I was amazed by the sight of this room on entering it, as it looked nothing like a library, more like a grand drawing room with grand piano and lovely furniture and a gorgeous polished floor.

I was immediately joined by a male spirit. This man was dressed in a long hooded cloak (very much like a monk would wear) and I felt that he was a holy man. What did strike me was the feeling of fear and that the man was hiding from someone. He was inside a little alcove that contained a chair, a window and two bookshelves. However, I could not make contact at this point as the spirit was simply reliving the events rather than being an intelligent spirit.

Service Corridor

I arrived at this long windowless corridor that had that looked as if it was straight out of a horror film. Walking along it I felt as if I was walking behind a female figure all the way down it. I was picking up the energies of a nurse in a building that was not a hospital. The reason I felt she was a nurse was I could feel the energies of someone who really cared about the well-being of others. It felt that she was also worried about people and that she spent a lot of time looking after people. When I get those kinds of feelings I know that I am communicating with a medical person from long ago. I later brought through her name was Joan Stevenson. Associated with this place was also a male spirit who I picked up the name Crowe.

This was not a voice as such; it was more the name had been placed in my thoughts.

Children's Nursery

This little room, off the Long Gallery, looked like a children's classroom or nursery. It had little desks and lots of toys that looked like they were from the Victorian era. The energy in this room was very fresh and mischievous and I believed the spirits here would move stuff and really tease anyone here alone. I felt that this room would contain poltergeist activity as there was so many of them. I could count at least seven spirits of children here.

Bedroom

In this bedroom I, and another person with no mediumship abilities, saw the figure of a man standing in the doorway. This man was standing watching us and told me that his name was Charles Carpenter and he was saying "Welcome" to us.

Psychometry

Chair in the alcove in the Library

I was asked by the people there with me to see if I could tune into the energy of the chair and find some information. On touching the wood I could feel that this seat belonged to someone very important. I will try and explain how this works for me personally. As I touched the object I could feel the emotions of both pride and arrogance. This led me to the conclusion to someone who was of great importance. He was arrogant as he didn't care about other people's opinions and he had so much pride as he knew he had achieved a lot. The other thing I felt as touching the chair was a great fear. I don't think this was the man's fear as it felt very much like my 'own' fear. This made me believe that the man was also someone to be feared.

Identity of the chair

I was later told that this was Nelson's chair and was taken from his ship. This made sense of the feeling that this was someone important and someone who should be feared.

Lump of Wood in the Library

On touching this piece of wood I was overwhelmed by the bad energy coming from it. The two main things I was picking up from this object were fear and death. How does fear and death feel in a lump of wood? This would be the question many people will want to know the answer to. Very similar to the feeling I was getting from the chair... I was scared. This means to me that people would always be scared when coming into contact with this item. As for Death... I could feel that many spirits were connected to this wood. They were there as they were taken so suddenly. I now knew that whatever this wood was it was involved in the death of people.

Identity of the Lump of Wood

I was later informed that this piece of wood was a chunk of wood from Charles I execution block. This verified the energies and feelings that I was picking up from the item. I would imagine that many other people would have lost their lives on this item, explaining why I picked up so many spirits connected with this wood.

My lasting thoughts on Kiplin Hall

This was a lovely old building and had a very cosy feel to it. I feel that a lot of the energy was actually coming from the objects within its walls. However, I also met many of the people who spent their lives in this fabulous building. The one thing about this location that stands out to me is the long service corridor. It is an image that is tailor made for a horror film. I feel honoured to have been given the opportunity to spend the night in this wonderful man-made creation.

Belsay Hall

Historical Background

Belsay Hall was constructed in 1807 and took a full decade to complete, designed by Sir Charles Monck (was once a Middleton). Sir Charles spent his honeymoon in Athens and fell in love with the Greek architecture so much that on his return he designed the new Belsay Hall in the Greek Revivalist style.

The Middleton family resided at Belsay Hall until 1962 when the family moved out and the site is now run by English Heritage and is open to the general public.

Paranormal stories linked to Belsay Hall

The Boy who loves frightening people

In the Dining room there is claimed to be the spirit of a boy child who loves nothing more than sneaking up on people and scaring them.

Man with Top Hat

Many people have said to have come across the ghost of a man with a top hat. The poor man tries to be friendly with those he meets but people still take to their heels and run.

Little Boy on tricycle

Many people have claimed to hear the laughter and noise of a young boy on a tricycle playing in the landing area at the top of the pillared room. Was this young boy killed here or did he pass from illness and choose to return to the spot he enjoyed so many happy times?

Poltergeist Activity

Over the years many people have reported things have been moved and hearing things banging from empty rooms. In the servants area doors are supposed to slam shut and even swing open.

Servants Area

This area is so scary that people say that members of staff refuse to enter alone.

Belsay Hall through the eyes of a medium

Pillared Hall

The outside of this location looks like something from Ancient Greece and on walking in the front door the Pillared Hall doesn't disappoint. I was met by the luxurious sight of marbled pillars rising from a marbled floor. This to me looked like the entrance to a palace. I wouldn't blame anyone for asking themselves if anything paranormal could possibly happen here. I found out straight away that this was not the case.

Something strange happened on entering the Pillared Hall... a voice spoke to me! There were no images and this wasn't a voice using my thoughts... This was a physical voice as real as yours or mine! The first thing the voice said to me was, "Welcome to my home." He also told me that his name was Charles Monck and that he was from the early 1800's. I have since found that this man was Charles Middleton (now Monck).

Dining Room

Like the rest of the building this room was bare apart from empty bookcases all around the wall. It would be easy to assume that this place was a library; however, I was shown it as a ballroom. Who showed me this? A lady who introduced herself as Louisa dressed in a beautiful ball gown. I was later informed by a historian that this Louisa was the wife of Charles Monck.

Upstairs Nursery

This room was empty when I entered it and there were no clues of its former existence. There was nothing in it, no carpet and nothing on the walls. On entering the room I immediately became aware of a young girl called Eleanor wearing a white dress and a ribbon in her hair in the room. She was sitting in the corner of the room playing with toys. This made me smile ☺. There were many child spirits in this room but the little girl was the one to catch my attention. It was such a sweet sight to see this young girl sitting playing with a little tea set all by herself.

During a séance later in the evening Charles returned and started whispering in my ear again, He told me that he got the idea of his house whilst on honeymoon. This was a perfectly normal thing to tell me... however, he then told me that he was on honeymoon for four year! This was later confirmed by a historian. He was also trying to tell me something about the gardens and Louisa but unfortunately I couldn't bring it through properly.

The Servants Quarters

The thing that struck me on entering this part of the house was the energy. There was a hive of activity as all the spirits went about their daily chores. I witnessed the spirit of a maid walking up the stairs. She was unaware of us... why was this? The reason for this is that they are not there in any intelligent sort of way. They are merely replaying an episode from their life. This can be something horrible that has happened or something very nice that has happened or simply re-enacting an event they would often do on this plane. In this case the maid was re-enacting her working life. She would have gone up and down those stairs hundreds of time each day. One other piece of phenomena that occurred was when I stood at the top of the stairs I felt dizzy and felt as if I was going to fall. This led me to believe that someone through time had fallen from this spot over the banister.

My lasting thoughts on Belsay hall

This fabulous old building had many layers, both physical and spiritual. From the beautiful entrance with its marble pillars and staircase to the shabby bedrooms right down to the crumbling filthy servants quarters. There was also lots of differing spirit activity. I would love to go back with a different team and see what more I could find about the fascinating inhabitants of this fabulous location.

Go now and enjoy your Paranormal Investigations but most of all HAVE FUN ☺

Blessings

Chris

XXX